Text © 2021 Jeff Zwiers
Illustrations © 2021 Reycraft Books

Special thanks to designer Faride Mereb.

Educators and Librarians: Our books may be purchased in bulk for promotional, educational,
or business use. Please contact sales@reycraftbooks.com.

Library of Congress Control Number: 2021902281

ISBN: 978-1-4788-7404-1

Printed in Dongguan, China. 8557/0221/17683

10 9 8 7 6 5 4 3 2 1

First Edition Hardcover published by Reycraft Books 2021

Reycraft Books and Newmark Learning, LLC, support diversity and the
First Amendment, and celebrate the right to read.

Reycraft Books
55 Fifth Avenue
New York, NY 10003

REYCRAFTBOOKS.COM

WHERE DO WORDS COME FROM?

BY JEFF ZWIERS

ILLUSTRATED BY SR. RENY

REYCRAFT
BOOKS

WORDS ARE EVERYWHERE.

But, where do words come from?

Do they come from . . .

or Wordbirds?

DO THEY COME FROM WORDBAKERIES?

WORDSTORMS?

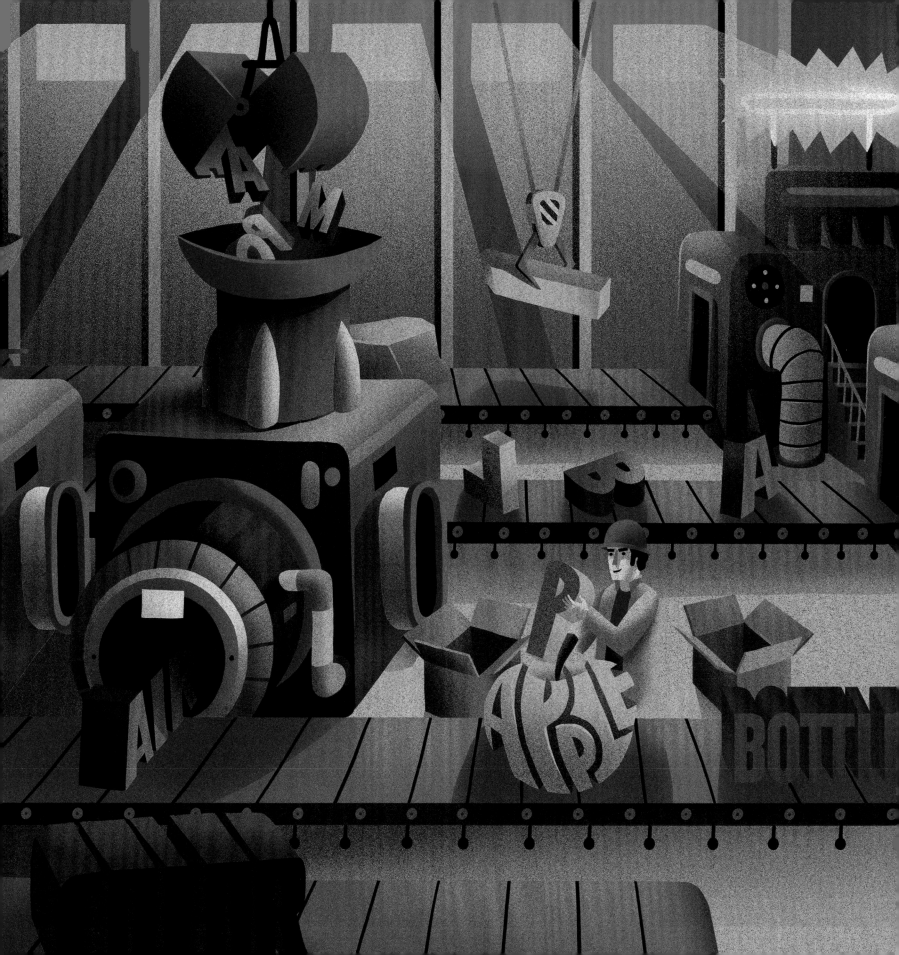

or Wordfactories?

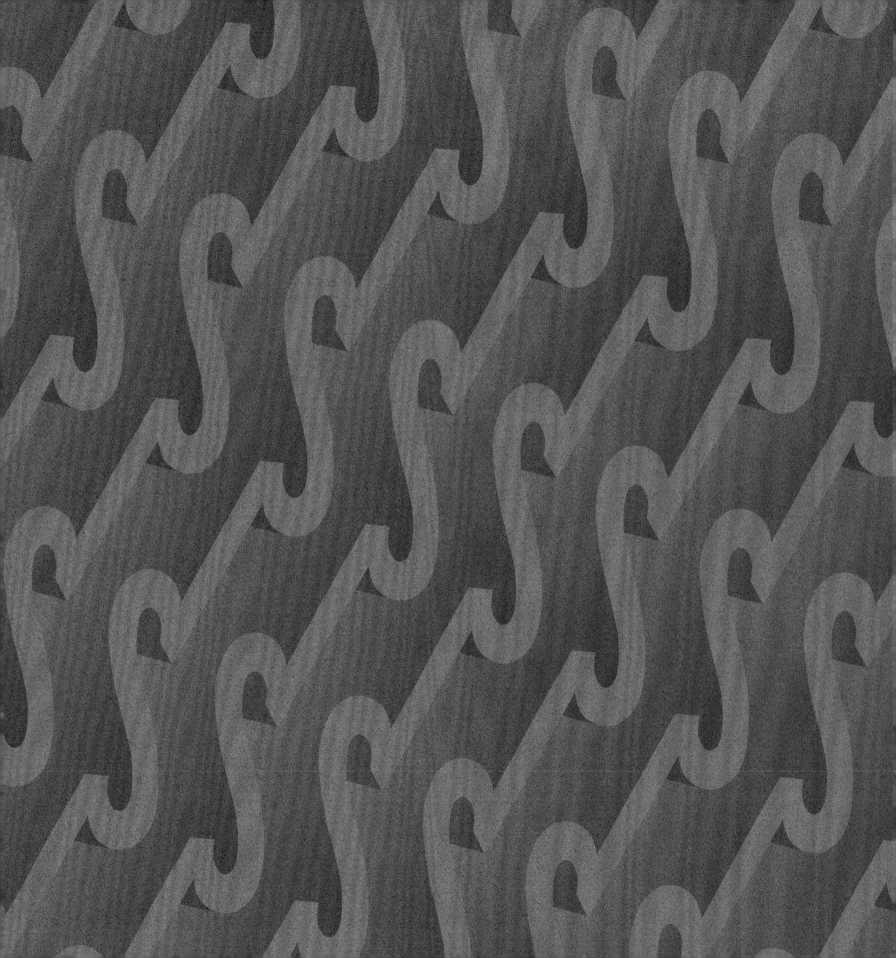

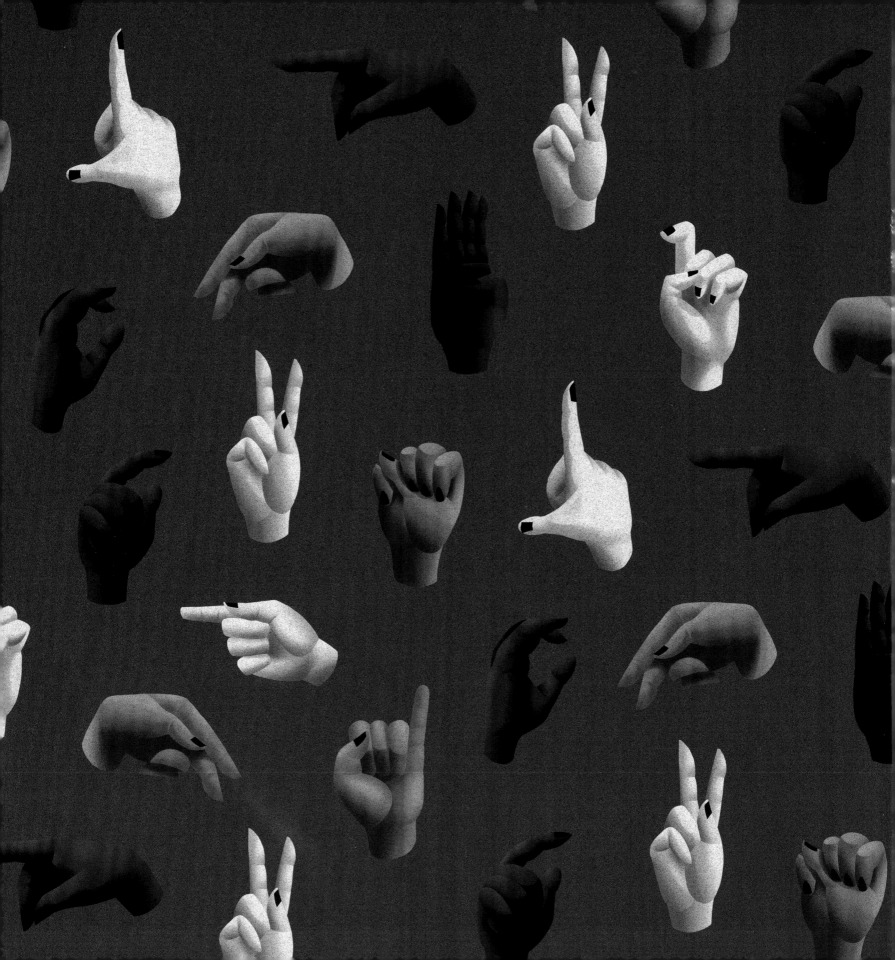

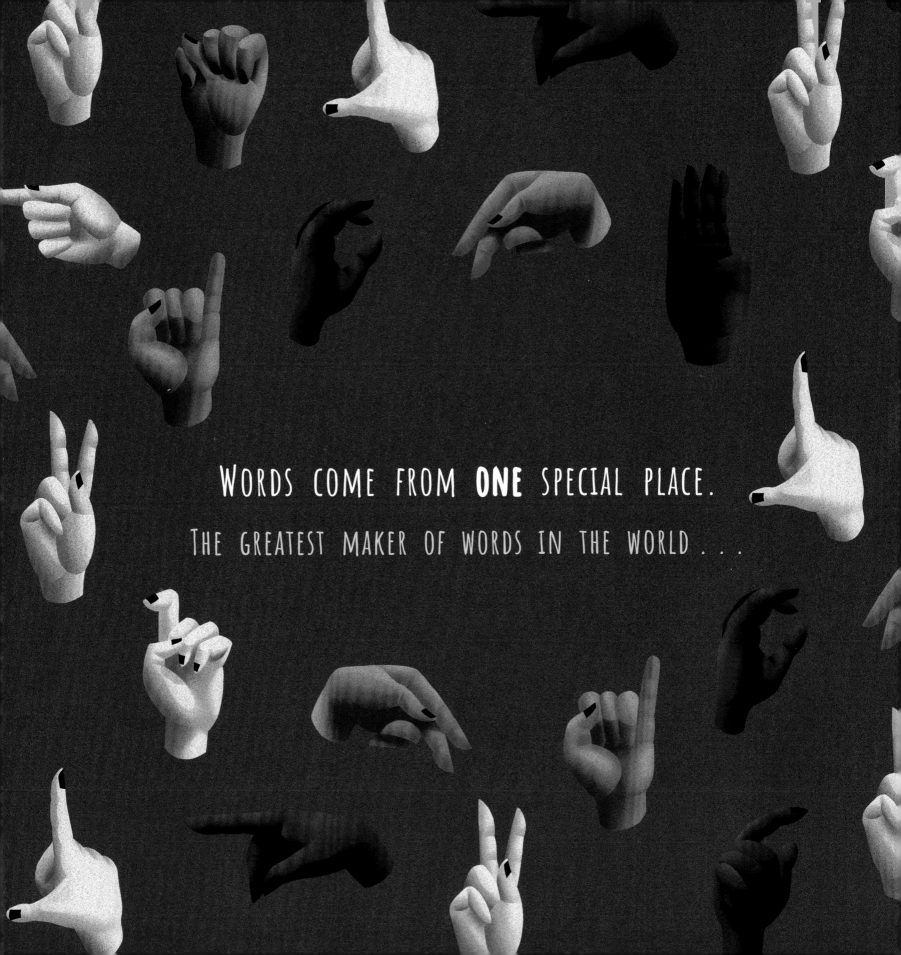

WORDS COME FROM **ONE** SPECIAL PLACE.

THE GREATEST MAKER OF WORDS IN THE WORLD . . .

YO
ALBERTO
BREIXO
ANNA
THANIA
MOHAMED
NIKITA
THANIA
SOPHIA

NIKITA

SOPHIA

JORDAN

MANUJ

aya   ROXA

TINO   FOUTINE   Mino

NAVANI

Raul   BAO   Sume

ROXANNA   IVAN

JANE   jengan   NEID

JORDAN   NIKITA

It's your turn to make up a new word.

Find or do something that has never had a name before.

Come up with a funny face.

Find a rock with a weird shape.

Move your body in a wild and crazy way.

Think up a new invention that turns broccoli into an ice cream sundae.

And then give your new thing a new name.

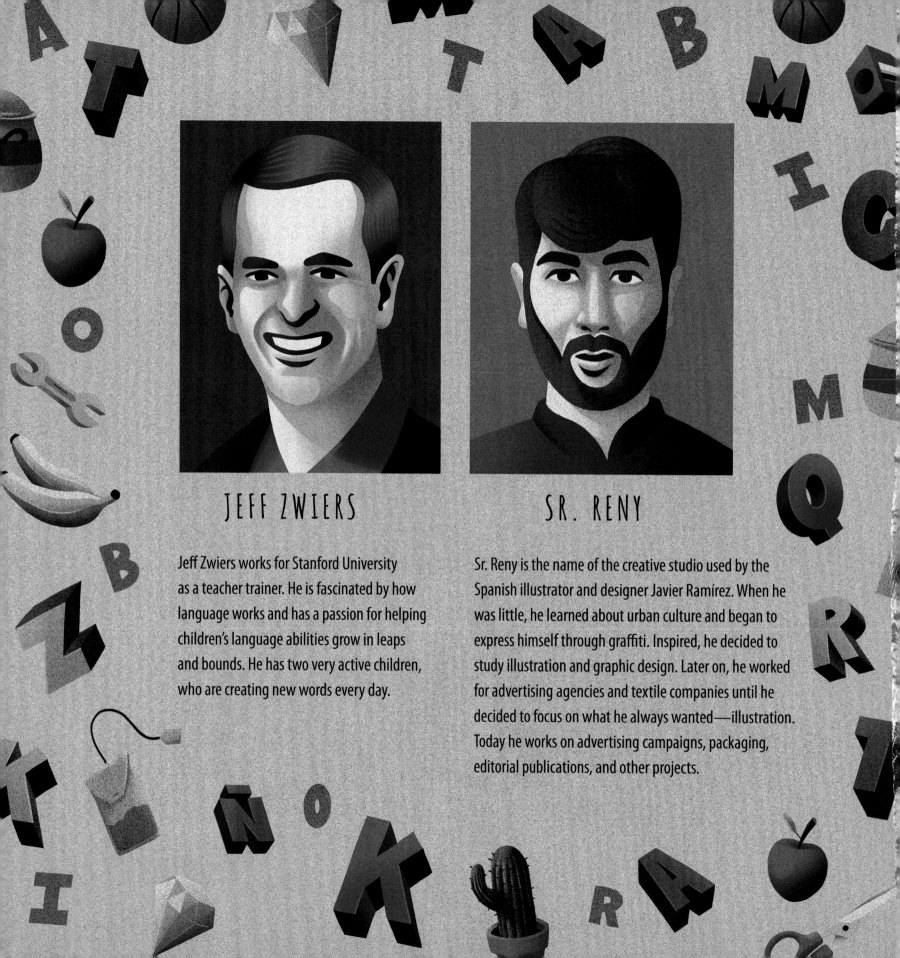

JEFF ZWIERS

SR. RENY

Jeff Zwiers works for Stanford University as a teacher trainer. He is fascinated by how language works and has a passion for helping children's language abilities grow in leaps and bounds. He has two very active children, who are creating new words every day.

Sr. Reny is the name of the creative studio used by the Spanish illustrator and designer Javier Ramírez. When he was little, he learned about urban culture and began to express himself through graffiti. Inspired, he decided to study illustration and graphic design. Later on, he worked for advertising agencies and textile companies until he decided to focus on what he always wanted—illustration. Today he works on advertising campaigns, packaging, editorial publications, and other projects.